The Pure Land

poems by

Ed Krizek

Finishing Line Press
Georgetown, Kentucky

The Pure Land

Copyright © 2019 by Ed Krizek
ISBN 978-1-64662-018-0 First Edition
All rights reserved under International and Pan-American Copyright Conventions. No part of this book may be reproduced in any manner whatsoever without written permission from the publisher, except in the case of brief quotations embodied in critical articles and reviews.

ACKNOWLEDGMENTS

In Hart's Tavern, *Piker Press* April 2018
Over the Phone, *Piker Press* May 2018
Daydream, *Eskimo Pi* July 2018
Alchemy, Piker Press June 2018
Loss, *Eunoia Review* April 2017
Service, *The Quiet Letter* June 2017
Demons, *North of Oxford* May 2017
Letter to a Buddhist Monk's Mother, *Young Ravens Literary Review* Summer 2017
Rabbits, *Literary Yard* February 2015
The Pure Land, *Young Ravens Literary Review* Summer 2017
Shrine, *Eunoia Review* April 2017

Thanks go to my teachers and all the bodhisattvas who have helped me learn something about poetry

Thanks also to Leonard Gontarek for his help preparing this book

Publisher: Leah Maines
Editor: Christen Kincaid
Cover Art: Photo by Nick Fewings on Unsplash
Author Photo: Ed Krizek
Cover Design: Elizabeth Maines McCleavy

Printed in the USA on acid-free paper.
Order online: www.finishinglinepress.com
        also available on amazon.com

                Author inquiries and mail orders:
                      Finishing Line Press
                      P. O. Box 1626
                Georgetown, Kentucky 40324
                        U. S. A.

Table of Contents

In Hart's Tavern 1

Over the Phone 2

Driving 3

Daydream 4

Alchemy 5

Dead Zone 6

The Rain Came Down 7

Loss 14

Augustana Lutheran Church 15

Last Meal 16

Waiting for Rain 17

Service 18

Demons 19

Letter to a Buddhist Monk's Mother 20

Rabbits 21

Chicken Livers 22

The Pure Land 23

Black Dog 24

Shrine 25

Today 27

Good-Bye 28

Message from a Fallen Angel 29

Elegy for Wes 30

For all the friends I have encountered on the path

In Hart's Tavern

I eat spinach and alfalfa sprouts
while wishing for a cheeseburger.
Salad is for rabbits. I feel good
about myself.

Marketing is the devil's work.
I have a graduate degree in marketing.
It turns out I am an easy mark
for hucksters. I wait for that magic feeling
the act of purchasing delivers.

Chilled to my innards I wish
for a warm body to mitigate the cold.

I consider the innocent
who have died in school shootings.
Satisfaction does not come
with arrest and conviction.
Nothing can bring them back.

Megan, the hostess, is reading
H.P. Lovecraft in Spanish.
She has just returned from
teaching in Costa Rica.
She wears her youth
like a lover's good-bye.

Over the Phone

His wife called.
He had a brain tumor.
I thought:
This is not good.

She phoned again.
It is malignant.
Surgery & treatment
to follow.
Hope in an experimental procedure.

A few days later I called & offered
to take him out for a day trip.
He declined.
I thought:
Soon there will be
no more time
& all the things that matter
will be long shadows
in the sunset.

There isn't anything to do
except pick a fight with
the unfair God
who allows these things
to happen,
where the best one can expect
is a draw & like Jacob
be blessed
when the long night
is over.

Driving

What joy that the sun is out!
The light casts morning shadows
along the parked cars.
There is a coating of spring
frost on my rear window.
When I turn the key
the engine starts
with a low-pitched throb.
The car moves slowly
over a yellow speed bump.
At the road turning right
or left is easy—
there are only a few cars.
As the street passes underneath
my seat, my mind relaxes.
Riding on a spring sunlit day
in the grip of expectation
all things are possible.

Daydream

All is quiet at the island dock.
Overcast day. I remove
my sunglasses as a jet drifts
away in the clouds. Glassware clangs
while being loaded into a black pickup.
Occasionally a car brought here
by the day, passes
or a golf cart rented by a tourist.
There is birdsong in the air.
I watch the locals.
A woman in frayed jeans
and flannel shirt is selling coffee.
Strong looking men
paint the bottom
of a fishing boat.
I can never find the courage
to give everything up,
live on the island,
grow a long beard,
speak to very few.
This persists
as I look out
at the calm water of the harbor.

Alchemy

In the drab light
with the sound of rain
a constant reminder.
I wait lying quietly
for the new,
hoping
to turn lead
into gold like JK Rowling's
sorcerer. I could live
as long as I wanted
and forget about the calcification
in my coronary arteries.

Dead Zone

The cold empty day looms
like a distrustful stranger.
I lie on the blue couch
in front of a fire
while considering.
Birds chirp in the trees.
They seem to wonder
where the sun has gone.
I hear them
without understanding.
All this time on my hands
and no desire to motivate
my actions. Perhaps I will fall
into the rhythm of dysfunction
and drift like a ghost myself
from thought to thought,
branch to branch.

The Rain Came Down
For my sister, Katherine

      1.

The rain came down
while ambition pulled us
inside granite and glass.
She brought
her own artwork—
a sacrifice to the gods of fame.
In the main gallery
was that kind of neutral abstract art
buyers read meaning into.
The casually dressed proprietor
was non-committal.
If you're an artist
just do your art.
He showed a Brancusi
he had stashed in a back room.
Was it more beautiful
than what she offered?

      2.

I want it all back!
she says.
She means the things
we gave away or sold.
I know it's the love she misses.
It remains a blurred photo
in her memory.
When conditions are right
she recalls things
she usually doesn't notice.
Most days fill with a deep sadness
that pierces her.
She longs for her father's voice,
her mother's touch.
They are gone.

3.
We left home earlier than planned.
That was good,
and there was time.
Time to see the house in Astoria
half a block from the El
where our grandparents lived
its red brick face hidden
by wooden siding.
Time to see Garden Bay Manor
where we lived until I was fourteen
with grass in the back yards now
instead of dirt.
Time to see the bungalow
outside Riverhead.
Beach front on Little Peconic Bay.
Time to see the big house
in Roslyn, always upscale.
Time to see the
former duck farm marked
by a thirty foot tall
duck, now a museum
owned by Suffolk County.
Two days driving.
Some places are worse
than we remembered—
some better.

4.
Our father's rose-colored gravestone
stands on a hill.
Over the years
the grave has received
my paternal grandparents
my uncle and my father.

There are two spaces left.
The empty spaces call to us
but we will not go.

      5.
The tree outside our old bedroom
is still there.
It's nicer than we remembered
grass on the ground
instead of dirt.
There are some new stores
on the commercial section of the block.
But the deli is still a deli
the pharmacy still on its corner.
I don't belong here now.
I light a cigarette.
Long dormant feelings rise up
from recollections.
Smoke
and tears
sting my eyes.

      6.
I rejoiced when a silver BMW
pulled up and
the current owner got out.
Welcoming and kind
she let us in.
Home again.
Many things were the same.
Many things were not.
Remodeled kitchen, baths
a fireplace where there wasn't one.
Green wall
color in strategic places.

The house is better than I remembered
yet the same.
Wooden stairs to the basement
built by my father
still there.
So too the walls
made of plaster
not sheet rock.
The red Japanese maple
I planted at age seventeen
has grown into a magnificent tree.
Modern art and furniture
that go with
the Meis Van Der Rohe-style architecture.

The current owner gave us coffee.
This house has good energy.
she said.
My sister replied
A lot of love was put into this house.
I never realized she knew.

Though happy with my current life
I miss the house.
When we lived there
I believed
my family had finally arrived
and would be part of Long Island royalty
forever.
My father died a year after we moved in.
My mother kept the house for ten years
then sold in a down market
for less
than it would have cost to rebuild.

7.
Look for the Big Duck!
my parents used to tell us
as we drove to the bungalow
outside Riverhead.
As kids we knew
once we saw the thirty foot high cement duck
built by a creative duck farmer
we were not far away.
Now it is a museum
owned by Suffolk County.
We stop.
The door is locked.
The clerk gets up
from behind the counter
lets us in.
At eleven-thirty AM
we are the first customers.
Few people go there anymore.
I buy a key chain
some refrigerator magnets
a canvas bag
all with pictures of the duck—
our shared symbol of childhood happiness.

8.
The Hampton Diner
is still there.
We ate lunch
before the drive back
to the present.
Jukebox gone
we ate without music—

talked
about the places
we'd just seen
what our lives
had been
long ago.
The waitress took
our picture.

     9.
Long slow drive back.
Traffic, tolls.
Memories jammed
in a place that hurts a little.
We traveled quietly
for hours.

     10.
One week today
she's been back at her home
in Italy with her husband
and children.
I think of her—

Here the sun shines
in a cloudless blue sky.
I shut the curtains
and turn on the lamp
in the darkened room.
Watch an episode
of a science fiction show
about a town populated

by geniuses
where something designed for good
goes awry in every segment.
The main characters
in this fictional place
always manage to solve
problems beyond
the capacity of most of us.
Still, there is always an issue
a dramatic thread
pulling the audience
forward into the next installment.

She is there and I am here.
Each of us continues our journey
separately yet linked by shared history.

Despite our desire
mistakes of the past
cannot be completely repaired.
We are left with
a longing
and the bittersweet.

Loss

1

Evergreens drop their needles
and leave a soft path of decay.
At the end
lies a black pool
surrounded by willows.
The long branches guide
raindrops onto the pool's surface.
The water is deep as grief.

2

Though we live
in denial
Death touches us all.
We must face
the inevitable conclusion
of our story. It is a novel
that seduces our attention
so we keep reading
even though we know
the end.

Augustana Lutheran Church

I served in a red cassock and white surplice,
held a gold lighter/extinguisher.
Lit the candles inside out,
extinguished them outside in.
The figure of Jesus
on the Cross which hung
in the middle of the candles
above the altar
my reference point;
Christ's light coming into the world,
Christ's light leaving the world.

The scent of burning wax
in my nostrils
as I walked down
the center aisle
behind the minister.

During the service I sat
in the special seat for acolytes
next to the pulpit,
certain I was in touch with God.

The communion wine
was changed to purple grape juice.
Mixed
with the body of Christ, it left
an aftertaste like Welch's jam on bread.

Last Meal

The last time I cooked for my friend
I broiled lamb chops, his favorite,
with sides of rice and a green vegetable
I don't remember. Vanilla ice cream
with home-made hot fudge sauce
ended the meal.

I think he was pleased with the chops,
though he wanted them medium rare,
and they came out medium well.

He was in the process of dying, slowly,
hanging on to every second.
When he asked why I made lamb chops,
his wife answered for him,
Because he thinks this might be your
last meal. Oh, was his reply.

As a volunteer
with Traveler's Aid, sitting
in the mausoleum-like train station
with stone walls and vaulted ceilings,
he told a confused traveler
that if she didn't know where she wanted to go
he couldn't help her get there.

He died a few weeks after that meal.
The minister gave a nice eulogy. Hopefully,
he got where he needed to be.

Waiting for Rain

Music of the running brook
echoes off nearby trees.
Gnats flying in my face
are blown away by a gentle wind.
I check my memory
the way one does a scab
to see if it's healed.
I do this every so often.
Yet you are still there
like a coating of dust
in my thoughts.
Rain clouds block the sun.
A cool breeze blows away
your image in my mind.
I pause while cricket-songs harmonize
with water.
I wait for rain
to wash me clean.

Service

The smiling waitress places a teapot
on the wooden table. I check
to see her name, Marie.
Glass mug waits
while the tea steeps.
It is an afternoon alone,
an afternoon for waiting
and reflection. The sounds
of clanking dishes, conversation,
and pouring ice cubes mingle
on their way to becoming white noise.
My afternoon turns to introspection.
I wonder how old friends are doing,
if there is life after death,
wonder if anyone from my past thinks of me.
Staring at the brown liquid in the mug,
I finally relax into contentment.
More patrons arrive and I fear displacement.
The day grows dark.
Night comes early
this time of year. Streetlights
are shining.

Demons
    After "Subway" by George Tooker

Flash like a bomb
on the dark hell. Unconscious
revelations. Ambush. Fear rises
when I see my shadow.
I try hiding, ignoring, running.
All paths block, barred.
I am a prisoner
of neuroses which cage me,
concrete and metal.
Where is the exit?
It seems there is only one way
out and Lucifer leans
at the foot of its stairs
holding a red carnation...

Letter to a Buddhist Monk's Mother

The days go by
quickly here. Up
at 3 AM for prayers
and meditation. At 5:30 we eat
breakfast of hot porridge,
and tsampa which is barley powder.
We mix the tsampa with yak butter
which offers a cheesy flavor.
There is no food after noon.
The days are spent in study.
We memorize the Sutras
as well as other Buddhist texts.
Later in the day we debate the merits of these
teachings with a partner.
My hair has been shaved off.
We do this as a sign of our commitment
to the sangha, which is our word for community.
It is true I sleep
on a wooden plank
with a four inch straw mattress. But,
there is calm
in the absence of distraction.
In times of stillness I see
the wrens that fly free outside the temple.
I hear their trills as I chop wood.
Before I came here I considered leaving
my soft bed, my corvette,
the parties with friends,
and you.
Still, this is the path I have chosen.
I must sweep the stones
out of the way
as I walk forward.

Rabbits

In the meadow
at the edge
of the wood
a rabbit lies
bleeding.
Entrails devoured
by a predator.

Everything has to eat.
At the final moment
the little animal's cries
resound across the meadow.
Worms and insects
collect their plenty.

The moon's
unnatural light
drapes the meadow
beside the trees.
Where are the rabbits?
They have retreated
into their burrows.
They are making love.
Soon more rabbits will come.
In the distance a wolf
howls.
Tomorrow the rabbits will
come out of the ground.

Chicken Livers

Cooking chicken livers is therapeutic.
Prepared with care,
according to a timeless recipe,
I transform a bloody mess
into a meal.
Never do I stop to wonder
how the chicken feels about all this.
Drunk on Irish whiskey,
I turn the burner on,
melt the butter,
and listen for the sound
of these entrails cooking.
When I move them around in the pan
I can almost see my future.

The Pure Land

Termites we make shelters,
of craving and desire
not sand and wood.
Instead of saliva
we hold them together
with lust for the measureable.
Roll the stone up the hill.
Amitabha! I want to go to the land of bliss.

An oppressed woman wishes to be free.
A poor man wishes for wealth.
A rich man wishes for love.
Amitabha! There is a place
where trees grant wishes
and sunlit sky holds rare and beautiful birds.
Fruit from the trees is sweet.
No one goes hungry.

We are caught
in an endless cycle.
Youth leads to old age, health punctuates disease,
birth results in death. *Amitabha!*
There is a place where suffering ceases
and all are awakened.
Soft light glows around contented faces.
Everyone is a Bodhisattva.

Black Dog

Depression is violence to the heart
seeking new avenues for sorrow
like a junkie searching for a vein
in a fervor.
A drug to dull the senses.
Take a sunlit day
and turn it black.
There is no point in fighting.
The dog always wins.

Shrine

I have collected totems in sixty-two years,
bought a wood and glass cabinet.
Framed in black an All-America certificate,
statuette holds the globe with Who's Who
written on it, framed the diplomas
which hang on the wall.
These are for him.

For her I saved the abalone shell
with its rose and green mother-of-pearl lining
her coffee cup and saucer,
a red rose painted on both,
and the word *Bonjour* spelled out in black.

While they dated my mother worked
at the New York Public Library.
Miniatures of its two white marble lions
(Patience and Fortitude) flank their wedding picture.
Their romance was tested many times.
He smashed a piece of the birthday cake
she bought him in her face. He didn't like the taste.
He chased her and my little sister in a tractor
threatening to mow them down.
In a fit of remorse he drove the turquoise
Volkswagen beetle into the canal. It got stuck
in the sand as I clung to the door handle
smelling the sea,
salt in my mouth,
trying to hold back the progression of madness.

Twenty-one years of marriage
until he fell from a six foot high scaffold
down a fifteen foot hole, breaking his neck.
She cried and cried at the news.

When I handle these symbols
finger tips brush off collected dust.
I look in the window of the wood
and glass cabinet
and close my eyes
on good times and bad.

Today

the azalea flowers have mostly died.
They hang wet and limp in faded reds
and pinks. White ones appear
as wet cotton at the ends of green branches.
Light on my face warms me.
With my belly full I look
into the forest for newness—
new blooms: greens and yellows.
As I walk through the woods,
rhododendrons with peach-colored blossoms
arise along the path. I trip over my own feet,
this day, this life.

Good-Bye

In front of a red brick building
in Queens lay a six foot by three foot patch.
There she planted purple and yellow pansies,
lavender hyacinth, white alyssum.
Flowers made her smile.
When she wasn't managing
mine, my sister's or my father's moods,
she worked on it.
Her garden an island
in the city's gray hardness.

When I became mentally ill
in mid-life all my lovers and friends
deserted me. She listened
to my paranoid rantings
about the CIA and
the guys who work on my head
without judgment
never giving in to despair.

When she got old, I moved her
into my two bedroom apartment
in a brick building outside Philadelphia.
Brought her meals on a tray.
She watched "The Price Is Right" religiously.
The people are so happy when they win!

As she lay dying, eyes closed,
morphine drip in her arm,
I held her hand.
Told her she was great, that I loved her.
I don't know if she could hear me.

Message from a Fallen Angel

Nothing ends my sadness.
Why do you love me?

Tarnished spoon serves bitter broth
while at the eaves doves hover.

Birds of prey kill for food.
The feast is hidden in the alcove of desire.

Beauty finds its place in living.
Divine musings drip from above.

There is something else for us to do.
Satisfaction comes in finding our way to the grove.

Ed says *Eat the apple and know what you must.*
Ignorance is not for you, my love!

Elegy for Wes

The phone rang
in early morning.
I didn't answer.
A message—
you died during the night.
Though I knew it was coming
your passing took my heart.

All of us, especially you, asked
How can this be?
You did everything right!
You took care of your son,
your sister, your father, your wife.
You helped me years ago
when I needed it.
You exercised daily,
had no vices.
Yet peering into the night sky
offers no answers. The time
you earned; time to travel,
time to love, has been cut short.

As months and years pass
I will remember you.
I will remember
the thirty-two years
we watched the Super Bowl together,
as each week of football season unfolds.
In spring I will remember
your photographs with each new flower.
And when I happen across
a beautiful place
I will remember how much
you loved life.

Ed Krizek was born and raised in New York City. Early in life Ed became involved in competitive swimming which served as a vehicle for educational and cultural opportunities. In 1970, Ed was named Honorable Mention on the Prep School All-America team in the 400 Freestyle. He went on to attend The University of Pennsylvania, and Columbia University where he earned degrees in biology, education, marketing, and health administration.

As a result of a lifelong desire to write Ed began writing prose then moved to poetry. He has been writing poetry for over twenty years and has over eighty published works. With the help of different teachers and workshop leaders Ed's poetry has matured into its present form which aims to reach all readers not just the initiated.

Ed currently lives in Ambler, PA with his wife Caroline. You can see more of his work at *www.edkrizekwriting.com*. There you can view samples of poems and short stories as well as find links on how to obtain Ed's other books.

www.ingramcontent.com/pod-product-compliance
Lightning Source LLC
LaVergne TN
LVHW041509070426
835507LV00012B/1439